The Role of the Executive Secretary/PA

Financial Times Management Briefings are happy to receive proposals from individuals who have expertise in the field of management education.

If you would like to discuss your ideas further, please contact Andrew Mould, Commissioning Editor.

Tel: 0171 447 2210
Fax: 0171 240 5771
e-mail: andrew.mould@pitmanpub.co.uk

FINANCIAL TIMES

Management Briefings

Human Resources

The Role of the Executive Secretary/PA

CAROLYN GILLIGAN

FT
PITMAN
PUBLISHING

London • Hong Kong • Johannesburg • Melbourne • Singapore • Washington DC

PITMAN PUBLISHING
128 Long Acre, London WC2E 9AN
Tel: +44 (0)171 447 2000
Fax: +44 (0)171 240 5771

A Division of Pearson Professional Limited

First published in Great Britain 1997

ISBN 0 273 63197 7

British Library Cataloguing in Publication Data
A CIP catalogue record for this book can be obtained from the British Library.

10 9 8 7 6 5 4 3 2 1

Printed and bound in Great Britain

The Publishers' policy is to use paper manufactured from sustainable forests.

CONTENTS

PREFACE

Over the last 10–15 years, the role of the Executive PA has changed drastically for a variety of reasons. In this report, I have set out what these changes have been and how they have occurred.

My aim in writing this report is to define clearly the role of the PA today. The report contains chapters which are of interest to PAs/secretaries and Directors/Managers. Some chapters are relevant to both groups and some are dedicated to either PAs or Directors.

While this report is based on my own experience and knowledge, I have been careful to gain evidence from other executive PAs to ensure that the same changes and developments are occurring in other sectors, both public and private.

I would like, through this report, to help PAs realise and use their potential and Directors to understand the important asset they have in a well-trained and professional PA.

ABOUT THE AUTHOR

Carolyn Gilligan has been a secretary and personal assistant for over 20 years. She has worked both in large and small companies and in London, Glasgow and small provincial towns. She is currently employed as Personal Assistant to the Chairman of Eastern Group plc. She is a Member of the European Association of Professional Secretaries and a committee member of the Secretarial Development Network and regularly speaks at conferences on how the role of the secretary has changed.

Chapter 1

HOW THE ROLE OF THE EXECUTIVE PA HAS EVOLVED

My aim in this report is to clarify the role of the executive PA today, working at director level. I hope it will enable the PA and her director to understand how they are benefiting from the change in the role and how they can continue to benefit by releasing the potential available to them, thus ensuring that the PA achieves, both for herself and her director. Incidentally, I refer to the executive PA as 'she' during this report, as 99% of the holders of the position are women.

By the nature of the seniority of the people she works with, the work of the PA differs in its complexity from the work done by a secretary working at a more junior level. I have, as the title of this report implies, concentrated on the work of these senior PAs who work at the highest level in their profession.

The role of the executive PA has changed considerably over the last five to ten years. When the term first came into common use in the early 1970s, it was used as a fashionable way of describing a private secretary; in fact, the work varied little from that role. However, while the title has remained the same for 20 years, the work today's PA is involved in is far removed from the work a private secretary/PA was expected to do when the title was first introduced.

The PA today fulfils a management role with all the responsibility and authority that goes with it. Today's executive PA needs to be well educated and multi-skilled. Being able to excel at shorthand and typing is not enough – although it must be stressed that they are still a valuable asset.

It is important to explain how and why the role has evolved over the last few years. The introduction of new office technology in the late 1970s and early 1980s was thought to signal the end of the secretary, private or otherwise. It was widely thought that secretaries were a dying breed and that they would be almost totally replaced by technology. Everyone in the office would be able to produce their own correspondence; a machine which needed no holiday or sick pay would replace the secretary.

Nice idea though this was in terms of cost cutting, the reverse happened. The new technology certainly led to a change in the role; rather than oblivion, it led to a change for the better as far as secretaries were concerned. A new role started to develop which called for a different focus on the skills needed, changing from a sometimes monotonous and dull job to one where new skills and competencies were required.

New technology has transformed the role of the executive PA. Answerphones are a tremendous asset, but they cannot communicate effectively. Humans are needed to interpret and action the messages that answerphones take. The enormous leap from the manual typewriter to the personal computer has released the PA from much of the time-consuming work she previously carried out. The advances in photocopying and general data collection and collation have transformed the day-to-day work of the PA, leaving her free to use other skills which are now regarded as essential to fulfil the role successfully.

The competencies of today's PA are totally different from those of her 1970s counterpart. These changing skills have allowed the PA to expand her parameters and take on more pro-active tasks in the office, allowing her to become a true assistant to her director so they can work as a team.

It is useful to define the role of the executive PA in order to clear the muddy waters which still seem to surround this role. There is no doubt that it is becoming a very important position in any company whether large, medium or small, although the old-fashioned view persists of the PA as a 'jumped up' secretary who is paid more. One of the biggest problems encountered by the professional PA is this erroneous image. It is often perpetrated by those who are unjustifiably worried by the threat of a good PA.

The executive PA's role is to assist her director; she doesn't want take his/her place. If that is her aim, she should be making a move into management; she will not be effective in a support role if her heart isn't in it. I examine the career prospects of the executive PA in Chapter 10.

Despite the variety of negative influences, the executive PA role has developed into an important part of any executive team and the better the quality of the PA, the better the executive team will function and achieve. Regarding the PA as an overpaid and over-titled typist is a mistake which can be very costly to companies. I hope that through this report, all those concerned with the role, i.e. the PAs themselves and those who employ them and work with them, will realise that without a good professional PA, both their own and their company's success will suffer.

Chapter 2

SKILLS FOR THE EXECUTIVE PA

Training for all secretaries is a difficult area and for executive PAs it is especially so. Many directors feel that for their PAs to be in the positions they are, further training is totally unnecessary. This is not true. We all need to continue learning; there is never a point at which we know it all. Training is, however, given a very low priority in the secretarial area. Apart from the fact that it's thought to be unnecessary, there's also the difficulty of releasing secretaries from the office – covering for absent secretaries is always a problem, especially the more senior the positions they hold. It is virtually impossible for all the secretaries and PAs in one company to come together for training sessions and this denies them a very beneficial and cost-effective method of training. Thus they are often placed in situations for which they have inadequate and irrelevant skills and I elaborate on the sometimes serious consequences of this in Chapter 4.

The role the executive PA performs today requires a variety of skills and I now detail the ones I feel are most important, and why.

TIME MANAGEMENT

Without a good understanding of effective time management, the executive PA will not be able to achieve for herself or her director. She will wander about in a sea of chaos, wasting her time and that of others who work with her.

There are several aspects of time management. It does not, as many believe, just mean keeping a diary. Time is our most precious commodity; we know it is fixed and that there are only so many hours, days and weeks. Once gone, we can't get them back. For everyone, therefore, it is vitally important that time is well managed. The executive PA needs to manage not only her director's time and her own, but that of those she supervises.

Although time management is a skill which can easily be learnt, it is more difficult to implement. It has to become a way of life. Everyone has to be committed to it and everyone needs it to work efficiently.

Successful time management needs to encompass all activities. Diary management is very important, but time management should cover all the time available in each day and be used as a planning tool for the future.

The executive PA should not just be thinking of this week. Her role is to plan ahead, so she should always be thinking about future activities. Good time management can only come from discipline – done well, it improves efficiency and creates a more professional image within the office. The PA needs to take control of both her own and her director's time and not let time take control of them. There are many time management courses specially designed for secretaries and they address the special situations PAs are in.

OFFICE MANAGEMENT

The executive PA is responsible for managing her director's office, which calls for a variety of skills to ensure that the office runs smoothly at all times. She should leave her director free to concentrate on his/her job. Directors do not want to have to worry about day-to-day minutiae – they should be able to rely on their PAs to do that.

The PA should be responsible for and take control of all the purchasing within the office, which means she should be aware of the office/department budget. Purchasing includes all travel, hospitality, training, equipment, stationery and other necessary items. She should make decisions on their priority and be able to justify their expense. If necessary, she should be able to negotiate with suppliers and ascertain whether real value for money is being obtained. She is far more likely than her director to know whether suppliers are reliable and if they offer good value. If necessary, she should look into particular areas of expenditure and submit a well-researched report on how savings could be achieved. The PA should accept all these responsibilities and have the confidence to take decisions which affect the office overall. She must keep herself abreast of new products and services and recommend change if she feels it is appropriate.

Successful office management comes with experience and confidence. Certain aspects are teachable – such as budgeting and negotiation – and again, good development and training are the key to success in this area.

COMMUNICATION

For me the most important skill for an executive PA to possess is communication – she must be able to convey a given message clearly and precisely, both verbally and in written form. She should be able to express herself in such a manner as to be understood and respected; without good communication skills she will be unable to function efficiently and effectively. She needs to be able to convey both her own and her director's thoughts and actions without them being distorted. Chinese whispers is not a game to play in the office as it can lead to ghastly consequences.

The PA must be able to compose a vast majority of the correspondence that her director sends, taking into account the recipient of the letter and composing it accordingly. She must have a good command of English and be aware of the tone and content of both correspondence and telephone communication. She is the 'go-between' – it is extremely important that she understands this – and as such, must be concise and positive. An executive PA should spend the minimum possible time on the telephone – a time waster par excellence. No one wants to listen to long explanations on the telephone. All the called party needs is to be advised of the reason for the call, then left to deal with it. Good telephone technique is very important to the PA and she should ensure that this area of her communication skills is excellent.

The executive PA also needs to be able to communicate with her director. She needs to understand the parameters she is working with and, equally, to convey to her director what she expects. Without this basic communication, the director/PA partnership will either never take off or will collapse. For instance, how much does her director wish her to use her 'eyes and ears' in the company? Is she expected to be a sounding board? How much will the director confide in her and how does he (or she) see his future? I expand on this in Chapter 9.

DIPLOMACY

Diplomacy is an executive PA's middle name; she will have to be diplomatic and use the skills associated with diplomacy 90% of her time. She has to understand the atmosphere and undercurrents which are running through her own office/department and throughout the company. She has to be constantly tactful and think quickly about what she is going to say or, more importantly, not say. A wrong word or sentence can seriously damage both herself and her director.

This is a skill which is mostly inborn; some people are naturally tactful and others are not, although it can be developed through experience. The best way for a PA who has problems in this area is for her to consider what she is about to say and how it will sound before she says it. No one expects an instant answer to statements or queries. She should give herself time to think about the message she wants to convey and weigh up its impact. If in doubt, she should say nothing.

She must learn the art of thinking on her feet. I have found the following stock answers useful in a number of situations:

'I can't comment on that'.

'I can pass your message on, but I can't guarantee that .... will call you. I can't give a promise for another person'.

'I'll make sure your message is passed to the right person'.

'I can only advise you of company policy in this area'.

Diplomacy comes with maturity and experience, but it should never be confused with confidentiality. A secretive person is not always diplomatic and the two are very different. A PA who is too secretive is more of a handicap than an undiplomatic PA.

PRO-ACTION

The executive PA needs above all else to be pro-active, constantly thinking about how to improve the methods she uses in her day-to-day running of the office. She should always be thinking about how to improve efficiency and be cost effective.

She must be able to identify areas that need improving and work out a solution to that problem area – she must be able to see the problem through to the end. Her director, indeed any director, wants solutions, not problems. She must be positive in her role and be able to justify why she feels a certain area is a cause for concern and what should be done about it. If the PA has a problem in any area, she must be able to take the initiative and solve it, either on her own or with her director's help.

The reactive PA is or should be a person of the past. She must be innovative, creative and positive; her role is not to wait to be told to do something, but rather, she must anticipate and

act using her own judgement. Mistakes may sometimes be made, but these can be used as experience and learnt from. With more and more directors working away from their offices for much of the time, a PA must take this pro-active role or her office will slowly grind to a halt. She must be able to set her own priorities, work to her own agenda and be capable of judging what it important and what is not.

DECISION-MAKING

Coupled with being pro-active and taking the initiative is decision making. Both she and her director must accept that the PA is responsible for making many of the decisions relating to the office/department. They range from simple ones such as 'shall I open this letter marked private and confidential?' to the hiring of junior secretarial and clerical staff in the office. The level of decision making will obviously depend on the parameters agreed between the director and herself, but occasions will arise when she has to make a decision for which the parameters may not have been discussed. The PA should make her decision based on the facts she has available to her and carry it out in a positive manner. She will have to accept that she may make a wrong decision, but as I have said before, mistakes are learning experiences and in most cases are unlikely to cause a major disaster. If it is a decision which is likely to have a major impact on the company, she will have judged that it was a decision she should not make. Decision making comes from judgement and like many of the skills examined in this chapter, it comes with experience.

Those are what I believe to be the essential skills for the executive PA today. She must also be extremely competent in the basic skills of shorthand, keyboarding, telephone techniques and English. She needs to have a good in-depth knowledge of a number of software packages in both word processing and spreadsheets. I also believe she needs to understand the hard-ware she uses. She must be aware of the different disk drives available to her, how they function and where they are situated in her machine. Too many secretaries are unaware of the vulnerability of their personal computers and the information they file on them. They fondly imagine that by using a password, their work cannot be corrupted or viewed. This is not the case, and if their computers are linked to a network, anyone with the minimum of skill can look at their files.

So knowledge of how their own PC and their network operates is important and, coupled with the ability to understand software, they can utilise their equipment to its fullest capacity. PAs must be encouraged to experiment with their software, as many feel that if they haven't learnt

a particular aspect of the package, they can't use it. The best way to learn is to find out for yourself – most software packages are very similar and all operate logically – so they should be encouraged to have a go and see what they can learn.

I have mentioned shorthand because, at director level, it is still an essential skill – most directors require it. Most like to use it as it enables them to have a feel for what they are dictating. I understand from secretarial colleges that audio-typing is becoming less popular and that managers who in the past would have used audio are now much more likely to type their own work on personal computers and then have their secretary tidy it up and present it correctly. This in many cases appears to be much more efficient.

There are of course many more skills needed for the executive PA, but I have examined those I feel are the most essential at this level when coupled with the personal qualities of flexibility, a positive attitude, the ability to understand the work, customer focus and responsibility.

Chapter 3

THE SUCCESSFUL EXECUTIVE PA

Having examined the skills needed for today's PA, I now look at how these can be put into practice in the form of a successful career PA. I will call her Ann.

Ann had the usual education and left school with A-levels, but, not wanting to go to university, had no idea what career to pursue. She is an outgoing, positive person who has always enjoyed being involved in a variety of activities. She was looking for a challenging career where she could use her brain and be a member of a team and which would allow her flexibility in her choice of work place. She was also looking for a chance to use her good linguistic skills.

Ann took a private secretarial course as a means of gaining some skills with which to enter the job market. All the students on the course were post A-level, so the standard was high and the students were expected to achieve good skills and speeds. The course was also varied and interesting with many more subjects besides shorthand and keyboarding, including commerce, secretarial duties, marketing, presentation and law. It gave her a good insight into the whole world of the office, one which she had not seen before. At the end of the course, she gained a private secretarial diploma and decided she would follow her career through the secretarial field.

She easily found her first job and discovered her personality was well suited to the environment she was now in. She was flexible, able to work well in a team and had the intelligence to undertake all the new tasks she was given. She was soon able to prove herself in her junior role and her ideas and suggestions helped her to move into a more senior position. Once in this job, Ann realised she would need to continue to learn if she were to reach the top of the profession and she was therefore very keen to undertake further training. She was lucky enough to be able to do this partly through her company, who provided suitable training and partly through her own efforts during non-working hours. She quickly moved up the career ladder and in a few years was an executive PA in a prestigious company.

Why is Ann so successful? Was it just luck that she was always in the right place at the right time or is there more to being a successful executive PA? Having decided on a secretarial

career, Ann ensured that she gained a good secretarial qualification. Without this she would not be as efficient a PA as she has proved to be. She has used her skills, personality and intelligence to get to the top. She has had the courage to move from company to company when the circumstances dictated and knows that she will always be in employment. One of Ann's most important assets has been her ability to work well within a team; wherever a secretary works in an organisation she is always part of a team, large or small, and without this ability no secretary is really going to achieve her full potential. But Ann has used her skills and added to them as her role has changed over the years. She has seen the opportunity to enhance her jobs by gaining respect from her employers and proving her ability to take on more and more responsibility.

Ann has developed a sixth sense when dealing with others in her organisation. She has learnt over the years to anticipate and act before she has been asked so that she is often one step ahead, and this means she doesn't panic when asked to do something. She asks questions of others before her director asks her. She uses her initiative to good advantage, is often starting new projects and is involved in the changes in her company.

She knows that the majority of her work is highly confidential and respects that, but she is not secretive and knows that other secretaries and managers rely on her and her knowledge to do their own job. She is able to distinguish between information she should never pass on and that which others need to know. The good executive PA needs to be aware of how what she knows affects others and although she must always be discreet, she should never keep knowledge to herself just to make her seem important. The executive team in any company should always work together and it is important to realise that the enemy is usually outside the company – it is not other PAs and their directors. Ann has developed her intuition to enable her to be non-obstructive and this is valued by her colleagues.

Ann has one golden rule which has helped her image tremendously throughout her working life – she never asks anyone to do anything she will not do herself. She is respected for this and it makes her very easy to work with. She has a junior secretary who assists her and she always ensures that the junior is kept informed as much as possible on what is going on in the office, which means they can easily cover for each other and the office is always well run. She wants her team to be successful and she particularly wants her junior to progress within her career. She encourages her as much as possible and helps her to obtain the correct training for now and the future.

Because Ann is easy to work with, efficient and always smiling, others react in a positive way towards her. They help her as she helps them and this is very beneficial to both Ann and her

director. She can always gain necessary information if she needs it because of the good rapport and respect she has built up. Ann also realises that she is in her position to do a job and as a result, she sometimes has to ask others in the organisation to carry out tasks. They may not want to do them, but if they need to be done, she will insist they are. She knows she is not there to be liked 100% of the time, but rather to get the job done.

Ann is also a very important link between the employees and her director, a bridge which they can both use. She can keep her director informed about general issues worrying employees and the atmosphere in the company. Often no one else will tell, so the director relies on Ann. They trust each other and this leads to greater success for them both.

Ann has always been aware that personality is very important in her profession. The personality fit between a PA and her director is essential for the team to function well, for if there is no personal rapport, trust will not grow easily. Ann would never accept a job if she thought she could not work well with the person who was employing her.

Like all PAs at her level, Ann is responsible for managing the director's office, as her director is out more than in and does not want to be bothered with day-to-day trivia. The director leaves her to organise schedules for others in the office and therefore the time management skill which Ann has acquired through training and experience is one of her most useful. She understands that time is manageable and sometimes has to be firm with her director when making appointments. His/her main concern is getting to the right appointment at the right time with the correct paperwork – the logistics are up to Ann.

Ann's success as an executive PA has come from two main areas. The first has been her ability to analyse her continual training needs – she has never thought she needed no further training and so as the executive PA role has changed over the years, Ann has been able to change with it and add the skills now necessary to be successful. Coupled with this, she is responsible for her achievements by being pro-active and wanting to succeed. She has always wanted to be the best – being merely satisfactory is not good enough for her – and she is continually seeking to improve her methods and the way in which she performs.

The second area of her success comes from her ability to gain the respect and assistance of others. She has done this through being efficient, professional and effective. She always gives an outward appearance of calm and is never known to panic. She has learnt how to promote herself through her positive attitude and ability to offer solutions to problems rather than more problems. Others know they can rely on her. She will make decisions and carry them out with the minimum of fuss and without delay. If she is wrong she accepts she is and

accepts constructive criticism when appropriate. She learns from her mistakes and uses them to advantage, and so the thought of being wrong does not stop her being decisive.

Ann always helps a colleague if she can and is always willing to take on further responsibilities. She is not known to say no very often, but has the ability to do so assertively if she feels it is necessary. Her communication skills are well proven and this, combined with her assertiveness, make her an excellent assistant to her director.

Ann's success makes her a valuable asset to her director and the company. She enables her director to get on with the job he/she is there for without worrying about peripherals, and their team works well. It is important, therefore, that Ann is shown she is valued.

Chapter 4

THE UNSUCCESSFUL EXECUTIVE PA

While there are too few Anns about in the job market, there are still unsuccessful executive PAs working at quite high levels in companies both large and small. You may ask how an unsuccessful PA keeps her job – surely she will be moved on? It is not always that easy. Often it is not the PA who is at fault, rather her lack of training and career development.

I am going to call my poor unsuccessful PA Kate. Kate had a similar education to Ann. However, she was not so interested in achieving and got little out of other school activities such as music or games, being an individual who only participates if pushed. She left school before A-levels and on her school's recommendation, took a commercial course at the same local college that Ann went to. But her course was not so advanced as Ann's, so she only learnt shorthand, keyboarding, simple book-keeping and telephone techniques. She left college with good skills and speeds and immediately found a job in a typing pool. Kate is not unintelligent, but she has no ambition and can see no point in gaining further qualifications or undertaking further training.

Kate enjoyed the lack of pressure in the typing pool; she knew what was expected of her and she felt in control. Due to her skills, she was promoted to the position of department short-hand typist where she worked for a manager and his team. She enjoyed her new position and was very happy, but she wasn't given any training to help her with her new secretarial and administration duties. She had no training in diary or time management, no presentation skills and no confidence-building development. Because it was not offered to her, she saw no reason to ask for it herself, assuming that her existing abilities were enough. Her experience to date would get her through, she thought.

Kate was later promoted to the position of director's secretary. Again her company failed to recognise the difference between a shorthand typist and an executive secretary and she was neither offered, nor did she ask for, further training. This has left Kate in a job for which she has no real training and no real idea how to perform efficiently. She has been given no new skills although the job she is now doing is far removed from the job she started with. She has no idea how to relate to others and is convinced that everything she handles is top secret. She did not know her director until she started on her first day, had no idea whether they would be compatible and is in fact scared of him. Not a very sound basis for a good team.

One of Kate's biggest problems is that she has never worked for another company, so she is unable to analyse the situation and see that she needs additional training. And because she has not had to develop communication skills, she doesn't know how to approach her director to ask for assistance in getting to grips with her job. So Kate is left to her own devices and expected to get on with the job. Kate soon becomes extremely stressed, and those working with her find her increasingly difficult.

Her director knows there is something not quite right, but is too busy to pinpoint it and as she is no different from his previous secretary, who was with him for many years. He is still under the impression that anyone who can write shorthand and type can be an executive secretary. They can be, but only with the correct training and development. The director thinks that the overfull diary and the fact that he is late for everything and the office looks as if a bomb has hit it are because he is such a busy and dynamic person. He doesn't realise that it's due to the chaos which reigns around Kate.

Kate proves to be very difficult to work with because of the stress she is under and those around her have to contend with her bad temper and constant queries about paperwork she has already received. She moves paper from place to place without actioning any of it. She keeps all the wrong things and destroys the things she should keep. The window sills are piled high with files and magazines and she keeps all junk mail, apparently unaware that this should be immediately discarded.

She spends far too long on the telephone cancelling and rearranging appointments due to poor time management. She has to apologise and explain constantly and becomes even more stressed and bad tempered. Kate is incapable of making a decision, so simple everyday office management is a nightmare for her and takes hours instead of minutes. She constantly has to ask other secretaries what to do about a given situation and then debates their advice far too long instead of dealing with the problem. She has no confidence and passes every piece of paper to her director for him to deal with. Kate takes no role in office management, forcing her director to spend time on trivial matters which she should be dealing with. She telephones another secretary to say she is bringing her some (unnecessary) information, then wastes time taking it.

Because of her lack of confidence Kate is scared of making a mistake and will not broach any subject with her director. She doesn't seem to understand how her director operates and they have no rapport. Kate has problems dealing with the staff under her supervision and keeps them totally in the dark, since she is under the impression that everything is secret. This makes their jobs very difficult. When she goes on leave, she leaves copious notes which convey nothing to her stand-in.

This situation and many like it drift on for several years and you may ask why they are allowed to. Often it is because the company is unaware of how its secretaries should be performing and accept the stress as part of the more demanding business environment. They still believe that typists can be executive PAs. Also, the director who can do something about the situation is not always aware of how difficult the executive secretary is to work with; he/she may have no idea of how others feel about the PA as no one has said anything. The director may think it's just a personal clash; that all PAs are the same. Consequently he (or she) has no idea that his public image is being tarnished. A director's PA and how she behaves is often seen as a reflection of the person she works with.

Kate carries on as usual, makes too many appointments but no decisions and works in a muddle while being rude to others. She is neither supportive nor encouraging to her junior and is still unaware that she needs training. Kate doesn't realise she has problems, believing that all executive PAs are stressed and over-worked. In fact if Kate were efficient and organised, she would be able to knock several hours off her work schedule.

Her main problems, however, lie in her inability to communicate and liaise with her peers, both internally and externally. She has never initiated a new idea and has no notion of problem solving. Her peers find it very difficult, since although she is a lovely person, she's hell to work with and all she does is move from crisis to crisis. Panic is her middle name. She constantly worries, and if asked to do anything outside her normal parameters, messes it up. She is excellent at delegating tasks she does not want and uses her position to bully rather than communicate and liaise. Her peers dread hearing her voice on the telephone.

She is totally unsuited to this job, and it shows, yet her director seems unable to do anything about the situation. Other managers and staff cannot understand why he puts up with her inefficiency and unprofessional behaviour.

Kate is not a failure; she's merely in the wrong job. There are many Kates in the office and they are not doing themselves or their company any good. Kate has none of the respect and success of Ann and for her own sake should be moved to a more suitable position where the skills she does have can be fully utilised and she will be relieved of the daily stress under which she lives.

Chapter 5

RETAINING A PA

Retaining a good executive PA takes great skill, whereas keeping the not-so-good is easy, as they find it difficult to move on. There are many examples of PAs who stay with their directors for many years, but changes in the employment market make this less common. It is now much more likely for an executive PA to stay with one director for many years only if they move to a new company together.

There are many reasons why moving as a team has become more common. The main one is that once a good relationship has been built between a director and PA, they are both keen for it to continue and the director is delighted to have someone he or she knows and trusts in the new company. Once this trust has been built up, it is difficult to justify the breaking of a successful, professional team. This situation has many advantages and some disadvantages for the PA. For the director it is nearly always good news, for the reasons given above; for the PA it is not so good, as she must work hard at mastering quickly the organisation they have joined.

On the other hand, the PA is in a good position to negotiate her package from a position of strength, as long as she ensures that her own career is not being held back by her loyalty to one director. She must make sure she does not lose out in the long run on career opportunities and developments which may open up for her. She must also ensure that her pension and other long-term benefits will not suffer by several company changes.

Good PAs move for a variety of reasons and in the present job market are difficult to retain. I go more deeply into the current market situation in Chapter 10, but want now to explore some of the ways in which companies can retain their successful executive PAs.

A small percentage of companies don't see this as a problem as they are still living in the days when typists were confused with secretaries. Until they realise the difference, they will be unable to attract and retain good secretarial staff. They must understand that executive PAs are made from good secretaries who need suitable and relevant training and a secretarial development plan. Companies who do not offer this will find it increasingly difficult to retain good secretarial staff.

There isn't a large pool of good secretarial staff in the market place waiting for jobs, so retention at all levels is very important. I concentrate on the executive PA and how to retain her either in her present job, or by allowing her to move into a management position. Good executive PAs are a valuable asset and make very good managers in other areas of a company.

Directors and their companies need to address the following questions when thinking about retention of PAs:

- why do I want to retain my PA?

- what can I offer her in the way of
  development
  training
  remuneration
  benefits
  job satisfaction?

- how can I ensure she will want to stay with me?

WHY DO I WANT TO RETAIN MY PA?

When a director realises that he (or she) wants to retain his PA, he must ask himself why – what does she offer that is so important? The director must look at his or her own position and see how she enhances it and what makes the partnership they have work so well. Every director/PA team is different, but they are all built on a mutual understanding of the other's expectations and agendas. Trusting in each other is, as I have mentioned before, a major part of this relationship. It is normally this trust and the way in which a successful team has been created which makes retention a real issue. No director wants to lose a PA who they value and respect, although they must be careful not to hold their PAs back: retention is also about keeping good staff in the company as a whole.

Directors have to ask themselves the question 'how will I feel if my PA hands in her notice to go and work elsewhere?' If they are unhappy with this idea, they must find out why she is leaving and whether they can manage to keep her. Often by the time a PA has found a new job, it is too late; she will have already felt that there was no future for her with her present company, or that she was undervalued. However, for those directors who want to keep their PAs, either in their own team or within the company, there are several options open.

WHAT CAN I OFFER MY PA TO RETAIN HER?

Job satisfaction

Like every other employee, a PA seeks job satisfaction; in fact this is one of the most important issues for her. An unhappy, bored and frustrated PA will almost certainly 'vote with her feet'. Therefore the more scope the PA is offered in her job, the happier she will be and the more she is likely to stay. The parameters will to some extent depend on her own ability, but if she is capable of relieving her director's workload, she should be encouraged to do so. A PA is very rarely after her director's job, but she should always be looking at ways in which she can make her superior's life less stressful. This expansion of the scope of a job leads to development.

Development

This can be a very useful tool in the retention of PAs. The successful PA will always be looking at ways in which she can develop both personally and professionally. Some will want to remain as PAs and be looking at ways in which they can develop in that role, while others will be looking at progress into management. No PA can ever say they cannot develop further; even PAs to Chairmen of top companies need further development and they should be actively seeking it. Their role is constantly changing and without career development, they will fall behind.

For retention purposes, offering development plans and opportunities to widen a PA's horizons is a positive action, because if their current company doesn't offer it, she is very likely to move to a company which does. Many companies now use their development plans in job advertisements. More and more companies have specific secretarial development and training programmes which cover all secretarial grades and offer job progression. This leads to training.

Training

Personal and professional development can only be achieved with on-going, relevant training. The myth that PAs do not need further training, that they should have the skills they need before they join is a very out-dated view and companies which subscribe to it will have problems retaining and recruiting good secretarial staff.

Different PAs require different training depending on their experience, but with assistance from their company's secretarial development manager, if available, their own director and other executive PAs, they should be able to define their own training needs. External courses are excellent networking arenas and will give PAs positive ideas and the ability to put their new skills into practice.

One area which training should cover is advanced technical knowledge – software, for instance, is changing all the time and PAs need to be kept abreast of current packages. In addition to this are management skills, finance, budgeting, business administration, presentation, public speaking and, if needed, the skills mentioned in Chapter 2.

Remuneration and benefits

I place this last as, contrary to many beliefs, it is not the biggest motivator for PAs. It is obviously very important, but the nature of the role and the personality of the PA make it less essential than job satisfaction and respect as a valued member of a successful team. However, remuneration needs to be looked at carefully in the changing job market and in view of the development of the PA's role over the last few years.

Most PAs will be aware of their director's remuneration packages, but not so many directors will know what their PA's salary and benefits are. Many companies still grade their PAs and secretaries according to their director's/manager's positions rather than individually. Every PA does a slightly different job and each of those jobs should be evaluated separately. In companies where this has been done, the majority of PAs and secretaries have had their salaries increased.

The executive PA, like everyone else, wants to be properly rewarded for the job she does and to have her status recognised. It must be accepted that she carries out an important role in the company structure. I explore her position in the organisational structure in Chapter 8.

Using remuneration and benefits for retention purposes can be beneficial to all. It is very important to examine what is happening in the market both locally and nationally, especially if the company is based within commuting distance of London or one of the other major cities. Salary scales are traditionally higher in London, but it is interesting to note that the differential in the secretarial field is shrinking. I give salary guidelines in Chapter 7.

Although the market rate is a good basis for setting a PA's salary level, other factors should also be taken into account. Is the company large or small? Is it national or multinational? How easy is recruitment and retention – do you have a high turnover of secretaries? If the executive PA's role has not been evaluated it is worth doing this, as it will indicate where she should be placed on the salary scale and also give a good feel as to what tasks she should perform.

The package of an executive PA should reflect how important she is to the company and her director and where she fits in the company organisation. If retention is a real issue, her overall package should be examined; she may be interested in other benefits rather than just salary and these can be used if the company operates a tight grading system. They can include free health care, non-contributory pension scheme, company car, share options and many others. An executive PA will almost certainly move to another company if she feels undervalued. If she is good, she will have no problems in finding a job elsewhere.

If a PA has decided to move to another company, it is always difficult to change her mind. Companies should always be looking at how to ensure that PAs are happy with their situation.

Chapter 6

RECRUITMENT

THE EMPLOYER'S VIEWPOINT

Replacing PAs who leave either permanently or on maternity leave can be a time-consuming and difficult task. A strategy plan needs to be drawn up to ensure that all avenues are covered and a suitable replacement found as quickly as possible. All the methods of recruitment need to be examined, as they all have advantages and disadvantages, and several criteria need to be established at the outset. If these are confused or left to chance, problems will arise later. The more information available at the start of the search, the more successful it will be.

Several questions should be asked before embarking on a search for a replacement PA:

- What is the budget for the recruitment process?

- What is the time scale available? This often depends on why the present PA is leaving. If she is going on maternity leave, several months are available. If she is leaving permanently, one month is probably her notice period.

- Are you looking locally or nationally?

- Have you a clear idea of the job and person specification? A change in PA may lead to a different emphasis being put on the role.

Setting a budget for the recruitment process is very important, as without one it can turn into a costly business. It is useful to obtain information on costs from agencies and newspapers. Agencies will also be happy to carry out testing, both of skills and personality, if no in-house facilities are available.

The choices available are internal recruitment, employment agencies, newspaper advertising, search consultants and personal recommendation/word of mouth. The method chosen will depend on the budget available, but all have plus and minus points.

Whichever method you choose, you will need to have compiled the following in order to obtain maximum benefit from the selection process:

- **An accurate job description**. Do not use the one that the previous incumbent of the job had. Look afresh at the job and what it entails; it may look quite different. You should ask the present PA to help you compile the job description as there is probably much more to the job than meets the eye.

- **A personal specification**. This should be a profile of the personal qualities and qualifications sought. Again they may be different from the qualities of the present PA.

The issues noted above need careful thought, as the more detail available at the start of the process the better chance there is of having a selection of suitable applicants. Figures 6.1 and 6.2 show examples of a job description and a personal specification respectively. These will obviously differ depending on the size and type of company and the seniority of the director, but the main elements remain the same whatever the individual case.

The executive PA role today demands a high level of education, preferably of at least 'A' level standard. Her previous experience should also be considered, although one should not have too strict a criterion for this as the candidate's personality and abilities are more impor-tant. It is, however, unlikely that anyone under 28/30 will be experienced enough to be a PA at main board level in a large company, although in a smaller company, a younger candidate may be very suitable.

A decision will need to be taken on whether the position should be offered internally, either by advertisement or by direct approach to suitable candidates. This has the advantage of conveying a good, positive message to junior secretaries within the company and boosts morale. Even those who apply and are unsuccessful will gain experience and confidence from the process of applying and being interviewed for a more senior position, although those who are unsuccessful should be counselled for reassurance on their future. They should be given advice on how to improve their prospects should another vacancy become available. Their lack of success may arise from something they had not considered and which they were not aware was a shortcoming. As part of the counselling process, advice should be given on further training, either skills-based or developmental, which may benefit them.

JOB DESCRIPTION

JOB TITLE: **Personal Assistant**

REPORTING TO: **Chief Executive**

SCOPE: **To provide administrative support to the Chief Executive and assist him/her with his role. To manage the Chief Executive's office and supervise his secretary and chauffeur.**

Responsible for the day-to-day correspondence of the Chief Executive's office.

Responsible for diary management and scheduling of appointments and meetings and arrangement as required.

Responsible for supervision of junior secretarial staff in the office – delegating as appropriate and ensuring they receive suitable and necessary training.

Responsible for categorising and delegating mail in an appropriate manner.

Responsible for all hospitality, travel and accommodation of the Chief Executive.

Responsible for the management of the office and the purchasing of all services and goods as required.

Responsible for ensuring that Chief Executive's suite is always in good order.

Responsible for allocation of director's meeting rooms and ensuring they are always clean and tidy.

Responsible for organisation of lunches the Chief Executive hosts on the premises.

Responsible for liaison with all outside charities and companies who Chief Executive is involved with.

Responsible for liaising with chauffeur.

To research and prepare appropriate reports on agreed subjects when required.

Undertake any training or development which is considered appropriate.

Undertake any reasonable task required as and when necessary.

Figure 6.1 Draw up a fresh job description for the new applicant.

PERSONAL SPECIFICATION

JOB TITLE: **Personal Assistant**

REPORTING TO: **Chief Executive**

SCOPE: **To provide administrative support to the Chief Executive and assist him with his role. To manage the Chief Executive's office and supervise his secretary and chauffeur.**

1	Customer focused	19	Intuitive
2	Flexible	20	Confident
3	Responsible	21	Ambitious
4	Diplomatic	22	Relaxed
5	Pro-active	23	Competent
6	Positive	24	Resourceful
7	A-level or higher standard of education	25	Enthusiastic
8	Good sense of humour	26	Organised
9	Reliable	27	Loyal
10	Assertive	28	Meticulous
11	Trustworthy	29	Analytical
12	Decisive	30	Open-minded
13	Adaptable	31	Likeable
14	Cheerful	32	Accurate
15	Co-operative	33	Efficient
16	Able to liaise at all levels	34	Successful
17	Professional	35	Healthy
18	Supervisory ability	36	Self-assured

Figure 6.2 The personal specification may change for the new PA.

Internal promotion is more likely to succeed where a secretarial development and training programme is in place, as it will have created a structured career path for secretaries and exposed junior secretaries who show potential. A company should always be aware of secretarial turnover; if too many senior secretaries and executive PAs are *in situ* for too long, good junior secretaries will leave the company to gain promotion and further experience. Indeed, if you recruit from outside, you may be gaining secretaries who see no career prospects in their present companies.

Companies which are committed to recruiting internally face great problems if there are no suitable candidates, and will be forced into recruiting someone who is not ideal. They will then need to provide relevant and proven training as soon as possible to ensure the candidate is able to undertake the role expected.

I would like to reiterate here that if internal promotion has been successful and a secretary has moved from working with a senior manager to a director, it is important that she receives appropriate training for her new position. She will be expected to use skills as an executive PA which she may not have used before. As I explained in Chapter 4, if she is under-skilled, she will be put under stress, the whole office will suffer and she will under-achieve.

If a company has no suitable internal applicants and is able to recruit externally, one of the recruitment methods mentioned at the beginning of this chapter must be used. It is important that all applicants are given a full job description and details of the remuneration package, plus any other relevant details when they first apply. Remember that the selection process goes both ways: you are considering her and she is considering you and your company.

Search consultants/personal contact/word of mouth

I have grouped these three issues together because it is often through personal contact that a likely candidate is noticed and approached via a search consultancy. Using a consultant allows anonymity and enables all the details about the candidate to be obtained before she knows who is interested in her. If, however, a suitable candidate is known through professional or social contacts, a direct approach can be made and a company can save itself a consultancy fee. Indeed, through the excellent networking systems now operating in the secretarial world, PAs themselves often know of good PAs who would be suitable. They also have the advantage of knowing how professionally they approach their job and how they are regarded by their peers.

This method of recruitment can be very successful as more is known about the candidate than can be judged from a written CV and an interview. Also, the PA will only take the job if she is really sure it is the correct one for her. It can cost more, however. The PA may be on a higher salary than you anticipated paying and your approaching her will put her in a better bargaining position. But with the market the way it is today, with a dwindling supply of high calibre PAs, it is becoming more and more common practice. The downside to this is that they may also be approached by other companies, so be aware of this possibility.

Recruitment agency

As with a search consultant, a recruitment agency can be expensive, but it takes a lot of the hard and time-consuming work out of recruitment. It is always wise to obtain details of charges and what you will expect to receive for your money from several agencies. They will all offer much the same service, but one might suit your type of company better than another. In London there are specialist agencies and if there is one in your field, they should be approached, as they will have PAs with the necessary experience in your industry/profession.

Recruitment agencies can vary in size from the small independent to the large agency or franchise. It is often a good idea to ask your contacts in other companies if they have experience of any agencies and get a feel for how well they fitted the applicants to the vacancy. Beware of those who send anyone who seems somewhere near the specification. This is where it is very important to have detailed and well-defined criteria; any vagueness and some agencies will send you details of totally unsuitable candidates. One word here about employing temporary staff – I now always ask to interview them before they commence as this saves a lot of time and potential embarrassment.

When choosing an agency it is very important to meet the consultant who will be dealing with your vacancy as it will give you a good idea of the agency's style and image. It is also a good idea to find out what testing they will carry out for you, if any (some agencies will not undertake this task). Also, you should ask whether they will test computer skills; non-computerised skills testing will not give you a true assessment of the candidate. You should also ask them if they test for numeracy and literacy and whether they will undertake psychometric testing for you or not.

The main job of an agency is to provide you, the employer, with a list of candidates who match your criteria. If you feel that more than one agency is needed because of time constraints or because you wish to make the vacancy available over a large area, the fees will be

larger, but you will have more chance of finding suitable candidates. If the agency/ies are not sending you the right type and calibre of candidates, tell them, or you will waste both your own and the candidates' time.

Another aspect you need to discuss with an agency is whether they will advertise your vacancy and if so, how, and what extra costs this may involve. If you advertise through an agency, you must consider whether you want your company name to appear. Never let them advertise unless they have your approval. The other important thing you need to know is what their refund system is if they should provide an unsuitable candidate, and how many months a candidate is guaranteed for.

A good agency will shortlist six to eight candidates for you to interview. They should provide full background details on them and up-to-date CVs, as well as notes on interviews which they have conducted with the candidates and why they feel they are suitable for the vacancy you have. You should also expect details on their availability, mobility, and salary expectations.

Agencies should be expected to carry out the majority of the initial fact-finding and sifting of candidates and then present you with a shortlist of suitable people. It is then up to you to progress the selection with structured interviews. These interviews will normally allow you to select, at most, two candidates who have the right personality fit with the director they will work with and then it will be a purely personal choice on behalf of the director and the candidate. Sometimes a candidate may feel that she cannot work successfully with the director. They must both feel they like each other enough to work together well as a team. I certainly have never taken a job, however good, if I have felt I could not get on with the director I am to work with.

Agencies vary in the rates they charge, but there is little difference between London and provincial agencies. They all charge on a sliding scale according to the annual salary of the vacancy and the percentage they charge rises with the salary. As a general guideline you should expect to pay between 15% and 22%. This charge should include testing of candidates, but some may charge extra for advertising. All offer a refund if the candidate does not prove suitable. They will all differ in how their refund system works, so it is advisable to ask for details of this when choosing an agency.

The cost of recruiting an executive PA on a salary of £20,000 will cost in the region of £4,000. This makes selection of the right PA very important as a mistake could be expensive in both time and money.

Advertising

If you have very well-defined criteria and the time and resources to use newspaper advertising, this can be a very successful and reasonably cheap form of recruitment. One of the problems of local or even national advertising is that you are unlikely to be anonymous, but some companies use job advertisements as a way of advertising what they are doing and how successful they are, so it is not always a bad thing. Press advertising will also require your company to have enough staff to deal with the response. This can be a large task and you have to decide at the outset as to whether you will reply to all applicants.

You will also have to allocate a member of staff to read through all the applications and decide which to send application forms to, again a costly exercise. Remember, too, that approximately 60% of the applications are likely to be totally unsuitable or unreadable, even if your advertisement is well written and defines the criteria you are looking for. Often an advertisement for an experienced executive PA will attract applications from college leavers or second jobbers.

The writing of the advertisement must be done with care and can take time, which must be costed. You will also have to negotiate a rate with the newspaper and decide whether to include your company logo, which is more expensive unless you advertise regularly. You must also pay regard to the laws governing employment advertising.

Local and national advertising can yield excellent results and will probably enable you to find a suitable candidate for your PA position, as well as supplying useful CVs for any other vacancies you currently have or may have in the near future. For this reason, you should keep them all.

If you advertise rather than use an agency, interviewing will take much longer. First you have to select a long list from the written applicants. I have found it useful to try to contact applicants on the telephone as you will gain much more knowledge of them this way than from their written applications. Having interviewed people on the long list, you then have to compile a shortlist for the director to interview and select from. All this takes time, and you will have to be conscious of time restraints: you may only have one month to find a replacement. As most PAs will have to give one month's notice, you are unlikely to have a hand-over period.

If your company is seeking a really top calibre PA, it will be worthwhile advertising in one of the quality newspapers such as *The Times*, either on your own account or through an agency.

Although this is costly, it will be worth it in the long run if you really do want the best. Career PAs regularly look at the appointment sections in these papers to see what is available and to keep up to date on current salaries. Often, many who currently travel to London may be tempted by a more local job. These newspapers are also a very good guide to the national and local market.

If you decide on advertising your vacancy it is advisable, if politically possible, to give salary guidelines, as this will save your switchboard from being blocked on the morning the advertisement appears. You should always remember to brief your switchboard if you are advertising as they will have to deal with a mass of enquiries even if you stipulate that no calls will be accepted. Some candidates always try to show their initiative by short cutting the system.

Interviewing the shortlist

You need a well-structured interviewing system to turn applicants into successful candidates. Interviewing shortlisted candidates needs careful consideration. Before interviewing takes place, all shortlisted candidates should have been tested in any way the company requires. There is some debate on whether experienced PAs should undertake skills testing; they will have been working at this level for several years, so on the face of it, it would seem unnecessary. One side of the debate contends that to do so is an insult and that many will be put off if testing is required. Bearing in mind the role of the PA today, are speeds in basic shorthand and keyboarding skills that important? How much typing does the average PA undertake? The chances of her needing to type at speed and having the opportunity to do so without interruption are remote. The other side of the debate says that, in the interest of good recruitment practice, testing shows a candidate that the company is interested in her and her skills and for the candidate there is a 'feel good' factor.

I feel that testing is for each company to decide on when they are setting the criteria for and planning their interviews. If they do decide they wish to test skills, then all candidates should be treated the same, although this may cause problems if there is a mix of internal and external candidates. Internal candidates may feel that the company should be well aware of the abilities they have, and if their work is below par, perhaps the company should have taken steps to improve their skills. This debate will probably continue.

Whatever the case, if testing is to be carried out, it must be on the appropriate equipment. A company can't expect candidates who may never have seen a typewriter, or who last used one

15 years ago, to undertake a test on one. The typewriter is a machine of the past; it cannot possibly give a fair picture of a candidate's skill and speed. Testing for accuracy and speed should be done on the appropriate equipment, using one of the many software packages designed for the job.

As in all interviews a well-structured format should be used. Thought should be given to who will conduct the interview and whether you will need a long and short list. It is essential that the director who the PA will work for is part of the interviewing system, either alone or with a panel. It is also good practice to be assisted by a senior PA skilled in interviewing; she will be able to assess the suitability of the candidate from the secretarial viewpoint and is often more aware of what is required than either a director or personnel officer. She will add real value to the interview process as she is an expert in her field. Many companies are moving towards having a secretarial development and recruitment manager, normally an experienced secretary who has progressed into management and has interviewing skills.

The recruitment process can take several months; it will usually take more than one month, which is all most PAs have to give in the way of notice. The average recruitment time for an executive PA is two to three months because, apart from the selected applicant having to give notice, it is always difficult finding interviewing time in a director's schedule. A director will need to spend from 45 minutes to an hour with each candidate and with an average of four on the shortlist, scheduling of the necessary time will be difficult. Therefore recruitment should start immediately a PA hands in her notice. You will probably have to rely on temporary cover for a few weeks between your current PA leaving and your new one starting, but this is better than employing the wrong permanent candidate.

Once a candidate has been selected and offered the position, references must be taken up. It is always useful to have a personal reference as well as a professional one.

THE EXECUTIVE PA'S VIEWPOINT

We'll assume you've decided to move on in your career. You don't feel you are able to do so with your present company, perhaps because your director is retiring/has retired or you see no further career development where you are. What is the best way to tackle a job move? The first question you need to ask yourself is, what type of job should I apply for? You may want a change of industry, profession or even location. The more detailed your criteria when starting your search, the better the result. I always look on career moves as a project and make sure the whole process is structured and well defined.

Your first step is to ask yourself why you are looking for a change. There are many reasons, including those mentioned above, and each is as valid as the next. Once you are fully committed to a change of job, you must take the first step: setting out your agenda. Begin by looking at your CV. There are lots of rules for writing CVs but I detail only the most important here:

- **Write an individual CV for each job you apply for**. By this I don't mean you have to rewrite the whole CV each time. Make a template of the details that are universal, such as your personal details, your qualifications and useful relevant information. You can then write your career history to reflect the experience you have in relation to the job you are applying for.

- **Include only relevant information**. Employers don't need or want to know your whole life history. Full details of your last two or three jobs are sufficient, while others should just be noted with dates of employment.

- **Limit the CV to two pages of A4**. You should be able to give enough information in this space to indicate your suitability for the job you are applying for.

- **Be clear and concise**. Set your CV out in a way which will encourage employers to want to read it. When detailing your career history, always start with the job you are currently in and work backwards. Always check spelling and grammar.

I always feel it's worthwhile printing your CV on good quality paper. It shows that you give attention to detail and will say a lot about your personality to the prospective employer.

You will have to decide whether you are going to register with a recruitment agency or rely on responding to advertisements in the newspapers. I recommend both. Many employers don't use agencies and, likewise, some vacancies never appear in a newspaper.

When you register with an agency, make sure you choose one which is likely to have the type of vacancy you are seeking. Look at the vacancies they have and the salary levels they offer. If your experience is in one particular industry or profession and you'd like to remain in that, you should register with a specialist agency. This is much easier in London than the provinces, but you will be more likely to be happier with the results. Choose the agencies you register with carefully. Make sure they have a professional image and that they ask you for a detailed history. They should be able to counsel you if you are unsure about a change of direction. They should test your skills and conduct a thorough interview to enable them to 'sell' you to a future employer.

If they arrange an interview for you, they should give you as much information as possible about the company who are recruiting, along with a full job description and guidelines on the remuneration package – it's no good wasting time on interviews where the salary is not what you are looking for. They should give you guidelines on what to wear and how to present yourself.

It's also a very good idea to obtain as much background information as possible about the company before you attend an interview. You will be much more relaxed if you know what the company manufactures, sells, trades or offers in the way of a service. It is also good practice to try and find out something about the director who is recruiting. This may be more difficult, but you can often find valuable information in the local library. The more you know, the better equipped you are for a successful interview, so be prepared.

If you apply for a job which is advertised in a newspaper, you should send your CV with a short covering letter. Remember the prospective employer may have many replies, so the more concise and attractive your CV looks, the better. The easier it is to read, the more likely that it will be read. Always ask in your letter for a full job description and salary guidelines; again it is no good wasting time if the salary is not acceptable.

The same interview preparation applies and you will impress the selection panel more if you have thought in advance of some questions related to the company or organisation you are applying to.

You may be very lucky and be approached by a search consultant or company direct. However, after the feeling of flattery has worn off you should proceed with caution; although there are advantages to this type of approach, there are several factors to consider. You should carefully check the company who has approached you, consider carefully whether you are ready for a change and if so, whether this opportunity is the right one. Ask them why they have approached you and how they obtained your name.

The benefits of being approached in this way can be considerable. The recruiting company may have been unsuccessful in finding a suitable candidate through the agency or advertising routes and you have been recommended to them, or someone in the company may already know you. If this is the case, the company will have approached you because they feel that your experience is what they are looking for and that you can do an excellent job for them. Do remember though, that however good the job, you must be sure you will be able to work with the director who is seeking the PA.

If you are happy with their approach, and you are successful, the benefit of this system is that you are in a very good position when it comes to negotiating your remuneration package. Never be happy with what you are first offered; there is always room for negotiation.

You must always be aware of how job changes will affect your pension, personal health plans, any loans you have with your company and your holiday entitlement. If you have a personal pension plan, moving from one job to another is not a problem, but if you are in an occupational pension scheme, you may well need to take expert advice from an independent source. Always look at the total package on offer when considering a new job.

When you attend an interview, you are there to sell your expertise, experience and ability. Be positive, ask questions and if you do not understand something, ask for clarification. Find out if the job description is accurate and as much as you can about the company and the director you will be working with. Will you have an assistant? How will she react to a new PA in the office? Did she want the PA job? Are there any other internal candidates who may be upset by an external appointment being made? Why is the current PA leaving and how long was she in the job? Is there scope for progression within the company; how do they view their PAs/secretaries in relation to moving into other areas of the business? Is there a training and development plan? How do they feel about networking, both internal and external? How many other PAs/secretaries do they employ?

You must also decide whether your personality will fit with the director. Does s/he have a sense of humour, is s/he open, approachable and friendly, does s/he seem interested in you? If it can be arranged, it is of great benefit to meet a prospective employer twice. This way, you will each have a better understanding of whether the partnership will work or not.

If you are successful at your interview and are offered the position, you must be sure that this is the correct move at this time. You will have thought seriously already, but until you are offered a position, it is hypothetical; now is the time to really analyse if this is the next job for you in your career plan/progression. Having got this far, the answer is very likely to be yes, but you must be sure the whole picture looks right, especially if you will be leaving a permanent job.

Well done! You have successfully made the next move in your career. Now is the time to negotiate your remuneration package. Don't be afraid to do this – you are the PA the company wants, so you must make them realise you are not going to be undervalued. If they stick rigidly to their original offer, ask them to explain why. Perhaps they can add some benefits to the salary to make it more attractive. Ask when the first review will be and how

increases are negotiated. Do all employees receive the same percentage increase or are increases linked to appraisals? Find out about pension plans and how they operate, and also whether the company offers discounted private health and other insurance plans. Find out what your holiday entitlement will be and whether it increases with length of service. If the company you are joining has a grading system, how can you progress from one grade to another?

Chapter 7

REMUNERATION AND CONTRACT

Now that you have selected your new executive PA, a remuneration package will have to be agreed with her. Obviously to some extent, this will depend on your company's grading structure and how rigidly you have to adhere to it. Nevertheless, several questions need to be addressed:

- At what level should the basic salary be set?

- What benefits if any should be included in the package – which are standard and which are optional?

- Should the PA be on a trial period (say, for three months), with a permanent contract being offered at the end of this period?

As I mentioned in Chapter 5, remuneration is an important factor in recruiting and retaining PAs, so it should be looked at in depth at the outset. I would therefore like to examine the way in which PAs are paid and how this has come about over the years. Most PAs are graded according to the level of their directors and, due to the change in the role over the last few years, tend to be paid according to the functions they performed in the past, rather than the role they perform today.

PAs have both increased their workload and added to their skills, and in many cases have taken on tasks which were previously undertaken by middle management. Figure 7.1 illustrates how flatter management structures have led to this. To a large extent this has not been recognised as it happened gradually and during a period of recession. Now the role is being seen as a much more important one and therefore needs to be recognised as such. There has been a gradual move towards grading the PA according to the job she does rather than according to the position of her director. Many companies now carry out job evaluations on all PA and secretarial positions and in most cases these evaluations have led to salary increases.

35

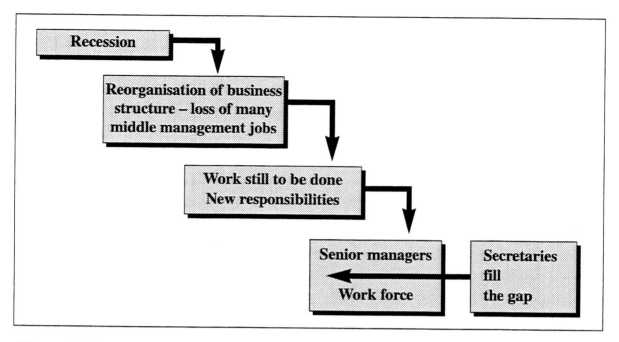

Figure 7.1 Secretarial staff are filling the gap created by a flatter management structure

It is common now for a PA to undertake research work and report writing and, if appropriate, present her report at board level. She undertakes project work, supervises support staff and prepares budgets. She is expected to be familiar with issues that affect her company and has an in-depth understanding of how the company works. She has to be familiar with problem-solving techniques to assist her director and herself in their work. The executive PA has become a middle manager. Some companies now realise this and PAs are graded accordingly, but there still seems to be a problem fitting them into the company structure. This usually becomes clear when they wish to progress within their company and Figure 7.2 illustrates this point.

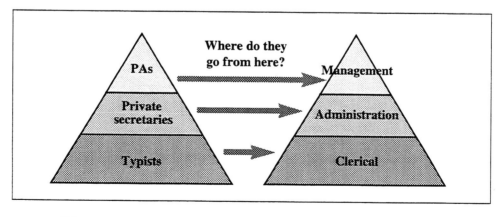

Figure 7.2 Where do PAs fit into the company structure?

A lack of precise definition of the PA's role can make setting a suitable remuneration package difficult. I give below some average figures for directors' PAs as guidelines. The salary you offer will depend on the current market situation in your area.

	London	Provincial
Headquarters of large company	£25,000	£17,000
Professional	£19,500	£13,000
Smaller companies	£23,000	£14,000

As a comparison, the average in the USA ranges from $35,000 to $50,000 (£23,000 to £33,000), with many benefits added to make a complete package.

The figures I have given should be used as guidelines, but it is interesting to note how salaries vary depending on types of company and that headquarters PAs based outside London are paid much less than their London equivalents. Could these differentials explain the current shortage of high calibre PAs?

In many cases, the job entails the same skills base and abilities whether it is in London or the provinces, so how is this differential justified? One needs to allow for travelling into and within London, but those who work in the provinces often have to travel long distances to work and normally by car, as public transport is limited.

Benefits and remuneration packages are starting to emerge and can include the following:

- company car (becoming more and more common – particularly in smaller companies with less rigid grading structures)

- non-contributory pension

- free health cover and annual health check

- share options

- mortgage subsidies

- season ticket loans

- personal loans

- gym/sports facilities

- five weeks-plus annual leave

- childcare vouchers

- luncheon vouchers/subsidised meals

- performance-related bonus

- discretionary bonus

- profit share

- long-term disability insurance

- flexitime

- paid overtime

- dental insurance.

A good PA will expect to be offered a salary which adequately rewards her for her experience and skill, plus some of the above benefits. And if your company does not offer her what she is looking for, another company probably will.

CONTRACTS

Most companies have a standard contract in place and this will be given to the PA. It is usual to contain the following clauses:

- normal working hours

- holiday entitlement

- remuneration package

- sickness

- grievance and disciplinary procedure

- commencement of employment and termination if contract is short term

- confidentiality agreement.

Because of the need for the personalities of the PA/director to be compatible, I feel it is always more acceptable to both parties to arrange a three-month trial period. This allows both sides to exit gracefully if they find they cannot form a partnership. It also allows a set review period when they can iron out any problems which have occurred and let each other know how they feel the partnership is working. It will allow a period when they can both judge the amount of responsibility and involvement they are happy with.

Whether a contract is given at the end of three months or on the date of commencement with the company, it should contain as much information as possible so that both employer and employee know what is expected of them. The more detailed and concise the contract, the less room there is for misunderstandings.

Hours

A contract should state working hours expected and whether they are fixed or flexible. If they are exceeded, is overtime paid and if so, at what rate? If overtime is not payable, is time off in lieu allowed and if so, does it have to be taken within a certain time?

Holidays

What is the holiday entitlement and how is it calculated? When does it run from and to (e.g. January to December/April to March)? Can holiday be carried over from one year to the next and if so, what are the rules attached to this? Does holiday have to be taken at a particular time (e.g. so many days at Christmas/New Year or in the months of July and August)? Is there a general shutdown period? Does the entitlement increase with length of service? Can the employee trade holiday for other benefits? If bank holidays have to be worked, how are they treated?

Remuneration

Clarity on this point is most important. A contract should state clearly the annual salary payable, when it is paid and by what method. All other benefits which have been offered should also be mentioned. In the case of private health cover it should be stated what level of cover is provided and whether it covers the employee only or includes her family. If a car is provided, its grade should be noted and the rules relating to private use included. Details about company and private petrol should also be shown. If the PA has use of a mobile phone,

the rules on private use and rental should be clear and likewise whether she is allowed to claim for business use of her home telephone.

Details should also be given about any other benefits which are included in the package, such as bonuses, profit share, performance-related pay and share option schemes, and how they are calculated. Details of any training or education the company has agreed to fund or assist with should be included.

Sickness

The company sickness policy should be outlined and details given on the allowed time off for sickness on full pay, half pay and when pay ceases. If the employee is unable to work because of sickness, the contract should specify the person she should contact and what documentation is required (e.g. when the company expects a doctor's certificate and when not).

Grievance and disciplinary policy

The PA should be advised of any policy which is in place and the procedure applicable under these policies. Also a note should be made of where a full copy of the policy can be obtained.

Commencement date

There should be a note on the contract of the exact commencement date of the employment and if it is only a temporary contract, the length of the contract and the finishing date.

Termination

The requirements for termination of employment by both sides should be clearly shown. A month is normal for PAs, although in some cases this is now being increased in line with their changing role.

Confidentiality

In common with other staff, the PA should have a confidentiality agreement included in her contract or as a separate document. In fact, because of the nature of her work, this is probably more important for the executive PA than for some other employees.

A contract should benefit both employee and employer in setting out the framework for them both to follow. And it should protect them both.

Chapter 8

WHERE DOES THE PA FIT INTO THE STRUCTURE OF A COMPANY?

The executive PA's place in the company depends a great deal on the size and type of company she works for and her own individual style and presence. I will explain this with regard to small, medium-sized and large companies separately, as her role in each, although equally important, can be very different.

SMALL COMPANIES

In small companies a good PA will almost certainly have a high profile and an influential role. She will normally work for both the Chairman and Chief Executive and will therefore offer a route to both these offices for other employees and directors. She will normally have much wider parameters than an executive PA in large companies, but her job will essentially be the same, requiring the same skills and attributes. How adept and successful she is at her job will have a significant impact on the whole company.

A PA in a small company is, as in every company, an 'ear' for the senior directors, keeping them up to date on all that is happening in the business and the general atmosphere and morale. She will be expected to deal with many extra responsibilities and with the kind of tasks that larger companies have whole departments to deal with. She will become involved in and responsible for arranging board and executive meetings, the administration of the whole office, possibly the personnel function, catering, organising the cleaning and facilities management as a whole, transport and other organisational aspects of the company. Her real role may well be that of office manager and she will find that she is often the person other employees rely on for projects and research they require.

She will certainly play a role in the recruitment and training of junior secretarial and clerical staff, either on her own or working in conjunction with the department who recruit staff. The executive PA in a small company will have to be a true all rounder and an excellent team player, willing to take on all responsibilities and tasks asked of her. If she succeeds and is good then she will be highly valued by both staff and directors. She has a much more difficult role to fulfil in many ways than an executive PA in a large company.

The downside is that she will probably be paid less for a much more complex job and the chances of advancement into management in the company will be limited.

MEDIUM-SIZED COMPANIES

The executive PA will have a more defined role in a medium-sized company as it is likely to have personnel and company secretarial departments. Nevertheless, she will still have a varied workload and will often be asked for assistance by specialist departments. She will probably find herself much more involved in the work of the Chairman and/or Chief Execu-tive, depending on whether she works for one or both of them. She may well find that she travels with them nationally and internationally. If she is confined to the company offices, she will probably know all about the projects they are working on and their views on them. She will certainly be able to answer queries if they arise as she is likely to have done some of the research and been involved in any reports or proposals prepared. Medium-sized companies use PAs as large companies use support departments. She will certainly be able to give sensible and accurate information when her director or directors are away.

She will expect to be and should be well briefed in every aspect of their work and able to take meetings should the need arise. PAs in this environment often have the greatest opportunity to progress easily into management and some all the way to director level. A loyal and successful PA in a medium-sized company is an asset who is usually well recognised. Her profile may not be as high as that of, say, the Chairman's/Chief Executive's PA in a small company, but she will have the advantage of being in a position to be noticed by those who can help her most to advance her career. Her position in the organisational structure may be less well defined, but it is a strong one.

LARGE COMPANIES

The executive PA in a large company has a much more specialised job, as she will normally only work for one senior director. But she will need every one of the skills outlined in Chapter 2, and more. She is also the most difficult to place in the organisational structure. She will most certainly be graded as a middle manager and paid accordingly, but she will lack status to some extent. Many will see her as 'only a secretary', even though the chances are she will have a secretary to assist her in her work, something not even many managers have today.

Each director in a large company will have a PA or private secretary to him/herself and the most senior PAs will have a secretary or clerical assistant to help them. The executive PA in a large company will need great presence and style to gain the status she is entitled to. Many of the middle managers in a large company will regard her as another secretary and not realise the status and power that she has. PAs are often regarded as 'dragons' who prevent their directors being disturbed, but this is an old fashioned idea and should not be allowed to continue in any company. Yes, they are there to protect their director, but he/she must be allowed to know what is going on in the company.

The work the executive PA is given and the role she plays depend a great deal on the PA herself and the director she works for. As I have mentioned before, setting the parameters is very important and can determine the role the PA plays in the company. Running the office of a senior director in a large company is a complex and, at times, difficult job. The secret is to make it look easy.

The PA may often have a junior secretary and a clerical assistant to organise. She may also have to organise a chauffeur's schedule, whether this be on a full time, part time or occasional basis. The logistics involved in transporting senior directors of large companies can be complex. The supervision of these employees and the way in which they carry out their tasks is a good indication of how good a PA is. The secretary is normally in place to assist the PA, but her role will depend on how she is managed. She may be asked to do just routine tasks or, if her PA is a good manager, she will be given specific jobs which she alone is responsible for. In some offices she will be expected to deal with all the correspondence and take all the dictation; in others the director may wish the PA to handle all his/her own correspondence. At the end of the day the PA must be the one who takes responsibility for the secretary and she must ensure that she is well motivated and happy. She must also ensure that the secretary has an opportunity to develop, and is encouraged to undertake suitable training.

This supervisory aspect of the executive PA role is a good indicator as to the PA's management abilities and whether she will fit easily into a more senior management position should she wish to. The management of directors' diaries needs to be excellent if they are to achieve all their objectives in the time available to them. The executive PA needs to have everyone working with her and to achieve this, she must be able to communicate well at all levels of the organisation. She will often rely on others to deliver briefing notes, statistics or information in order for her to fulfil her role.

The executive PA in a large company needs to have the ability to build up respect so that others want to work with her. She also needs to be able to create that relationship with

external contacts in other companies. For instance, she must be able to communicate and liaise effectively with travel agents, PAs in companies she regularly deals with and suppliers of goods and services.

An executive PA in a large company has a powerful position and may be loath to leave it and move on up the management ladder. However, she must remember that her power comes from her director's position and that if she has the ability, she should take opportunities open to her and develop her career as an individual. PAs can tend to stay in one position too long; they see it as their goal. There are several reasons for this. Some have no further ambition, others are neither encouraged nor helped to move into other areas, either internal or external, and some do not have the ability to progress further. It is never ideal for a senior executive PA to remain in the same position for too long as she will stagnate, and it brings career progression for junior secretaries in the same company to a standstill.

The executive PA in a large company is in a very good position to move into management; like all PAs, she is closely involved in the day-to-day management of the company and sees how it works at the top. She is also able to observe how more junior managers in the organisation operate and how successful they are. She has regular contact with all grades of management in a company and is in an ideal position to promote herself. The way in which she communicates and responds to them will influence how they perceive and consequently respect her.

A successful PA will be highly regarded in her company and is well placed to develop her career further. She should also remember that she is a role model for junior secretaries and as such, she must be aware that others will imitate her behaviour and attitude. She must always behave in a professional and positive manner.

An executive PA who is at the top of her profession has a wealth of knowledge and experience in her field and this should be utilised by her company. She should be involved in the setting up and running of networks internally and externally and encouraged to hand on her experience to junior secretaries via development and training programmes. All too often, executive PAs become isolated and office bound, which is no good for them or their directors. They should ensure that they leave their desks occasionally and become ambassadors for themselves, their directors and their companies.

PAs should network as much as possible. It takes time, but it's always worth it. Promoting the secretarial image within the company is something the executive PA is in an excellent position to undertake and she should be initiating creative ways in which this can be done.

Executive PAs in large companies are graded in such a way that although they may appear to be lower down the organisational structure than their equivalent in a medium-sized or small company, they do in fact have as much, if not more power and if they choose to use it, they can develop their careers as they wish.

It will become more difficult to fit the executive PA into the organisational structure as their role develops further over the next 5–10 years. There is a definite move to follow the example of the United States and introduce the executive assistant role. I explain this in Chapter 10.

Chapter 9

CHIEF EXECUTIVES –
HOW TO ENSURE YOU HAVE THE BEST PA POSSIBLE

I am writing this chapter for all chief executives and other senior directors. If you read only this chapter it should give you an opportunity to know your PA better and help her to develop her career. I would like to explain from the PA's point of view what she expects to give and receive from you.

You have reached the top. You are the best in your field, so you deserve the best PA possible to assist you. Have you got the best? If not, why not? What can you do to either make your present PA the best or replace her with what you need?

I have worked at Managing Director/Chairman level for most of my secretarial career in several types of company and I have seen the changes over the years in the role I have undertaken. I have used a flexible approach to adapt to these changes and am now at the top of my profession. During my career to date I have worked with ten very different directors, all male, and I have enjoyed working for every one of them. The relationship which the PA and her director builds is a relatively intimate one and if you do not feel that you have such a relationship with your PA, then I would suggest that something is wrong in the personality mix. You must feel that you can trust your PA to be discreet and honest and that she will never repeat anything she hears while working with you. You spend a lot of your time either with her in the office or talking to her on the telephone; therefore, for your team to work successfully you must feel comfortable with each other. If in any way she annoys you or you her, it will be apparent to those around you, and it will tarnish your image. Your PA will not give of her best if she feels that the relationship is difficult.

This is why selection of PAs is so important and why you can't leave it to someone else to choose for you. If the chemistry is right and you like each other, the team will almost certainly be successful. It cannot depend on your success alone. For this reason, you should give a lot of thought to the type of PA you need and want. It is no good having a very extrovert PA if you dislike that type of person and she will not fit in with your personality. Likewise, if you have a wonderful sense of humour which you use to good effect in your working life, then you need to have a PA who can respond to this and not be offended by your quips. Your choice will also depend on how much or little you like to delegate to your PA. If

you are not willing to allow her to become involved in your work, do not choose a graduate who is keen to develop her career further. You should think long and hard before setting out the criteria for your PA. Your choice will say a lot about you to your organisation and to the outside world.

You may move into a situation where there is an incumbent PA; either her last director has retired or has moved on and not taken her with him (or her) to the new company or has no new job to go to himself. Whatever the reason, it can lead to a difficult situation. You may not be suited to each other and once the situation is accepted, it is very difficult to disentangle oneself. As I have mentioned in Chapter 7, I strongly believe that, in the interest of both parties, there should be a three-month trial period in which the PA can judge her new director and vice versa. This will allow them both the chance to see if they can work together or not. If after this time they are happy with each other, a lot of time and money has been saved in recruitment; if, however, they find they have a personality clash, or work in totally different ways or cannot agree on the amount of involvement required of the PA, they can act positively before the situation becomes too difficult.

A trial period will allow either of them to bow out gracefully and give the PA an opportunity to review her career. A good PA will never be afraid of change and should always be able to find another position, internally or externally. She may be very happy to see you through your initial few months with the company, help you find a replacement and then leave to develop her career elsewhere. All this should be discussed before you take up your new position so that she is fully aware of what is happening; too many companies just assume their secretarial staff will be happy to do what they are told. This is not the case – they like to be consulted and advised if their jobs are to be affected. I've known companies where secretaries are told they are to leave one job and move to another without being consulted; where they and the manager/director they are joining do not meet until they start to work together. This is a far from ideal situation and leads to much unhappiness and demotivation.

If you are retiring or leaving a company and not taking your PA, you must consider the impact this will have on her. It is up to you to discuss with her what she is thinking of doing and whether she will need your help in moving within the company. You may find she has already been active in looking at her options, but she may need some advice from you. You should explain that your successor may bring his or her own PA, or may wish to recruit one when in place. The new director may well want your present PA to reapply and she may find this daunting, especially if she has been with you a long time and is out of touch with interview techniques. If she wants to stay in the job, you must arrange for her to receive advice on how to prepare for an interview and how to promote herself positively to your successor.

Where you are taking your PA with you into your next job, it is essential that you ensure that her loyalty to you is also good for her career. You must discuss her long-term goals and her overall career development. Is she growing with you or are you developing your career while hers is remaining static? It is also important she does not lose out in terms of pension or other benefits which build up over a number of years. If you value your PA enough to want to keep her with you, it is up to you to help her to negotiate a package with your new company, or even do this yourself. You should be satisfied that she is not disadvantaged in any way.

You are happy with your PA and she is happy with you; this is the best ingredient for a successful relationship. If the partnership is working, you are both probably doing all the right things. But are you aware of her plans and goals? Do you both regularly discuss your goals and targets? She cannot assist you fully unless you keep her well informed. She should know your aims for the coming year and how she can help you achieve them. I'm sure that if you work well together, you are already doing this, but are you helping her as much as she is helping you? Or are you quite happy for her just to deal with the routine matters in your office and not be too involved?

As long as she is happy with this situation, all is well – but would you know if things were not well? Is your relationship good enough for her to discuss problems with you and are you willing to discuss them? Most director/PA teams have regular discussions on goal setting and achievements which can lead to further training or more responsibility. The parameters you set out when you first became a team are constantly altering, as we live in a changing business environment and those who don't change lose out. So as your terms of reference change, so should those of your PA. Talk to her, encourage her and support her in what she does; you will get much more from her if you do. She will respond by being positive and relaxed. If your PA is constantly stressed and under pressure, something is seriously wrong in the office and you should find out what it is and remedy it.

A good executive PA is an excellent sounding board. She will normally have good, usable ideas and will certainly see the pros and cons of your proposals and projects. She is the ideal person to help you with research and project work as she knows how you react and what your opinions are and so can easily understand the type of information you are looking for. She will also normally know where to find it. The more involved she becomes, the better she will be at her job. The better she does her job, the more you will achieve, as she will be able to take more of your peripheral work and leave you to concentrate on the core task.

She will also be able to supply you with information about the atmosphere in the company and the state of staff morale. She should be used as your 'eyes and ears': part of her role is to

keep you well informed. She may sometimes find that members of staff are secretive with her, but she should nevertheless be able to glean the information she feels you should have.

Her career development should be seen as a reflection on yourself and your style of management. Just as a below-par PA can mar your image, a good one can be a positive asset. If she wants to remain a PA, ensure she is constantly updating her technical and practical skills, but if she has shown a desire to move into another area of the company, encourage her. Just because she is good and you have a wonderful team does not mean you should hold her back for ever. On the contrary, advise her and help her achieve her aims. If you hold her back too long she will eventually become frustrated and leave to join another company, so you will lose her anyway.

Your PA's role is to support you and run your office efficiently and smoothly while you're running the company. You're too busy for office management, so hand it all over to your PA, since she is perfectly capable of budgeting and organising the workload. Delegate as much as you can – believe me, she will welcome it. She may make mistakes, but she should learn from these and be happy to take constructive criticism, but she must be aware that she has your support and backing. If you listen to your PA and keep her well informed, you will have a calm and relaxed assistant who gets on with the job in hand in an effective and efficient manner.

If the partnership is not working and the idyllic situation described above is not one you recognise, what can you do? There may be a variety of reasons for this. You may have inherited an unsuitable or untrained PA; you may have progressed in your career, but your PA has remained static; you may have chosen the wrong PA. Whatever the reason, it is difficult to find a comfortable solution to the problem.

Is your PA always stressed? Is she short with others she works with? Does she try to blame others for her errors? Is she late with deadlines? Is she reactive, not pro-active? How often does she make suggestions? Does she have an untidy desk? Does she know where everything is? Is she always willing to take on new responsibilities? Does she repeat herself? Is she secretive?

If your PA is prone to any or all of the above, the first step is to talk to her and get her view of the situation. She may think her way of working is quite normal and blame it on her workload. Discuss with her how she would like to solve the problem, and if she does have too much work, offer her an assistant. Let her initiate a solution if she can, and action it, as she will learn a great deal from doing this. She may need training in certain areas and if this is the

case, the problems are easily overcome. Make sure she is given guidance on suitable training and that she arranges it sooner rather than later. Encourage her to take the time needed for the course or courses.

If the root of the problem is personality or lack of ability, the only real solution is to move her to another position within the company. But this will have to be done with great care. It may take time to solve the problem and it is often easier to let it drift rather than tackle it head on – but it will not get better without action.

You should not settle for second best when you need good assistance. Remember, a director with an inefficient and over-stressed PA is seen as having a weak team and this can be bad, both for the director and the company. You may well spend more time with your PA than you do with your family, so choosing and keeping the right one and having a good partnership with her is essential.

Chapter 10

THE FUTURE

The role of the executive PA has changed over the last few years and will continue to do so. These changes have been brought about by technology, business reorganisation and the redefinition of the secretarial role of all grades. They have been felt in several areas, but the real impact has been seen in recruitment, the skills and qualities now required and the secretarial market world-wide.

The secretarial market in America has also been changing over the last few years and it has become increasingly difficult to recruit and retain high calibre PAs/secretaries. There are several reasons over and above those I have mentioned. The most significant is the shift in women's employment in the last 10 to 15 years. Women can now choose from any number of careers, unlike the days when the majority of women had only teaching, nursing and secretarial careers open to them. This has meant that those who may in the past have become secretaries are now taking up other careers which offer more scope, progression and money.

To alleviate the problem, a new position has appeared at the top end of the secretarial profession, that of the executive assistant. This has enabled companies to recruit graduates with relevant skills into PA positions by enlarging the scope of the job they are expected to do. It is also an excellent way of keeping good PAs in the profession instead of them moving into another area of an organisation. The executive assistant is more likely to travel with her (or increasingly in this position) his director and stand in for him or her when appropriate. An executive assistant has more status than a PA and correspondingly more responsibility. They are in fact what a secretary was when the word first came into use in Middle English: a confidant who is empowered to act for another.

The expansion of the role in this way has increased and will continue to increase its appeal, thereby enabling the recruitment and retention of high calibre candidates in the profession. Other ways of attracting and retaining potential PAs need to be explored. For instance, companies should look at introducing structured secretarial trainee programmes to enable them to train either college or school leavers to the standard they require. This would also give the young secretaries of today a career plan that would appeal to them.

Those who are involved in the secretarial profession need to promote the value of the role more positively. This is already starting to happen through secretarial conferences, shows and seminars, and through secretarial development networks who are successfully encouraging companies of the desirability of networking and the positive effect this has on their PAs/ secretaries.

I would like to comment briefly on the secretarial market at the moment. At the time of writing this report, it has become extremely good for the PA/secretary, not only in London, but everywhere. There is a shortage of good PAs/secretaries and in some areas it has become a buyer's market in favour of the secretary. This swing has come about from the shortage of good quality entrants into the profession, the lack of executive PAs/secretaries with shorthand and the changes in the role itself. There aren't enough PAs with the relevant skills and personal qualities needed to be 'today's PA'.

This tightening of the market is leading to improved salary levels, particularly at the top. There has also been a move towards the payment of bonuses, either performance-related or discretionary, which enables employers to pay more to those who merit it. However, as I have explained earlier in this report, recruitment and retention is not only about remuneration and salary levels. Employers need to look closely at what else they can offer to ensure a continued supply of high calibre PAs and secretaries at all levels.